PRINCEWILL LAGANG

Startup Success in the Digital Age

First published by PRINCEWILL LAGANG 2023

Copyright © 2023 by Princewill Lagang

All rights reserved. No part of this publication may be reproduced, stored or transmitted in any form or by any means, electronic, mechanical, photocopying, recording, scanning, or otherwise without written permission from the publisher. It is illegal to copy this book, post it to a website, or distribute it by any other means without permission.

Princewill Lagang asserts the moral right to be identified as the author of this work.

First edition

This book was professionally typeset on Reedsy.
Find out more at reedsy.com

Contents

1. Introduction — 1
2. Startup Success in the Digital Age — 4
3. From Idea to Innovation — 9
4. Crafting a Compelling Brand and Effective Marketing Strategy — 14
5. Customer Acquisition and Growth Strategies — 19
6. Innovation and Adaptation in the Digital Landscape — 23
7. Financial Management and Sustainability — 27
8. Nurturing Team Dynamics, Leadership, and Company Culture — 31
9. Adaptability and Resilience in Startup Entrepreneurship — 35
10. Navigating the Startup Ecosystem — 39
11. The Path to Startup Success: Key Principles and Strategies — 43
12. Beyond Startup Success: Sustaining and Scaling — 46
13. Looking Ahead: Future Trends and Possibilities — 50

1

Introduction

Welcome to the dynamic world of startup entrepreneurship in the digital age. In an era defined by rapid technological advancements and ever-shifting market landscapes, startups have become the engines of innovation, shaping industries and changing the way we live and work. This book, "Startup Success in the Digital Age," is your comprehensive guide to navigating the exhilarating, yet often challenging, journey of launching, growing, and sustaining a successful startup.

In the following chapters, we will embark on a journey that covers every facet of the startup ecosystem. Whether you're a seasoned entrepreneur looking to fine-tune your strategies or a first-time founder seeking guidance, this book is designed to provide you with the knowledge and insights needed to thrive in the digital age.

The Digital Age: A Paradigm Shift

The digital age has revolutionized the way business is conducted, transforming the very essence of entrepreneurship. Startups, with their agility and innovative spirit, have emerged as key players in this new era. They challenge traditional business models, redefine customer experiences, and bring groundbreaking solutions to market. However, the rapid evolution of technology and consumer expectations has made this landscape both exhilarating and unpredictable.

The digital age has also democratized entrepreneurship, providing access to information, resources, and global markets like never before. It has leveled the playing field, allowing startups with innovative ideas to compete with industry giants. Yet, it also poses unique challenges, as competition is fierce, and the pace of change is relentless.

A Roadmap to Startup Success

"Startup Success in the Digital Age" is structured to be your guiding light through this exciting and complex landscape. Each chapter is dedicated to a fundamental aspect of startup entrepreneurship, offering a deep dive into critical topics such as ideation, marketing, financial management, team dynamics, adaptability, and scaling strategies. Additionally, we explore the human element of startups, the role of the broader ecosystem, and future trends that will shape the entrepreneurial journey.

The knowledge and insights provided in this book are designed to empower you to navigate the intricacies of entrepreneurship. By embracing innovation, fostering a resilient team, and adapting to change, you can position your startup for success and make a meaningful impact in the digital age.

A Continuous Journey

It's important to recognize that startup success is not a fixed destination but an ongoing journey. It's a path filled with triumphs and challenges, requiring adaptability, resilience, and a commitment to continuous learning. As you delve into the chapters that follow, keep in mind that your journey is unique, and every lesson learned, whether from success or failure, is a valuable part

INTRODUCTION

of your story.

We invite you to explore the depths of entrepreneurship, to embrace change, and to envision the possibilities that the digital age offers. With this guide in hand, you have the tools to embark on your own startup adventure and to make a lasting mark in the ever-evolving world of entrepreneurship.

Let's begin this transformative journey together and explore the myriad facets of startup success in the digital age.

2

Startup Success in the Digital Age

In the fast-paced and ever-evolving landscape of the digital age, startups hold a unique position at the intersection of innovation and entrepreneurship. As they strive to transform novel ideas into sustainable businesses, they face a set of challenges and opportunities that are distinct from those of established companies. This chapter will explore the essential elements and strategies that contribute to startup success in the digital age, shedding light on the key factors that can determine whether a fledgling venture soars to new heights or fades into obscurity.

1.1 The Digital Age Landscape

The digital age, characterized by the rapid advancement of technology and the pervasive influence of the internet, has revolutionized the way we live, work, and conduct business. With the advent of smartphones, cloud computing, artificial intelligence, and the Internet of Things (IoT), the opportunities for startups to disrupt traditional industries and create innovative solutions are seemingly boundless.

1.1.1 Ubiquitous Connectivity

One of the defining features of the digital age is the widespread connectivity that enables instant communication, information sharing, and global reach. The ability to connect with customers, partners, and remote teams across the world has transformed the way startups operate and market their products or services.

1.1.2 Data-Driven Decision-Making

Data is the lifeblood of the digital age. Startups have access to a wealth of information that can inform their strategies, guide product development, and enhance customer experiences. Harnessing data analytics is essential for staying competitive in this environment.

1.1.3 Accelerated Innovation

The rapid pace of technological innovation means that startups must continually adapt and evolve to remain relevant. This creates both a challenge and an opportunity, as those who can effectively harness these innovations can gain a significant edge.

1.2 The Startup Ecosystem

Within the digital age, the startup ecosystem has grown and evolved, creating a supportive environment for entrepreneurs looking to bring their ideas to life. Key components of this ecosystem include:

1.2.1 Incubators and Accelerators

Incubators and accelerators provide valuable mentorship, resources, and funding to early-stage startups, helping them refine their business models and accelerate growth.

1.2.2 Venture Capital

Venture capital firms invest in startups with high growth potential, providing them with the financial support needed to scale rapidly.

1.2.3 Co-working Spaces

Co-working spaces offer flexible, collaborative environments for startups to work and network with like-minded entrepreneurs.

1.2.4 Online Communities

Digital platforms and forums connect startups to a global network of entrepreneurs, enabling knowledge sharing and community building.

1.3 The Success Equation

Startup success in the digital age is influenced by a combination of factors, including a clear vision, innovative product or service, effective execution, and a deep understanding of the market. The success equation for startups can be summarized as follows:

1.3.1 Vision

Start with a compelling vision that defines your mission, values, and long-term goals. Your vision will serve as a guiding star for your startup throughout its journey.

1.3.2 Market Research

Thoroughly understand your target market, identifying pain points and opportunities that your product or service can address. A deep understanding of your audience is essential for tailoring your offering to their needs.

1.3.3 Innovation

Innovation is at the core of startup success. Your product or service should offer a unique value proposition, setting you apart from competitors and attracting early adopters.

1.3.4 Execution

A well-executed plan is crucial. This involves building a strong team, managing resources effectively, and meeting milestones to reach product-market fit.

1.3.5 Adaptability

The digital age is characterized by rapid change. Startups that can adapt to shifting market dynamics and emerging technologies are more likely to thrive.

1.4 Navigating Challenges

While startups have tremendous potential for success in the digital age, they also face a myriad of challenges. These may include:

1.4.1 Funding

Securing adequate funding is a persistent challenge for startups, requiring innovative approaches such as bootstrapping, crowdfunding, or pitching to investors.

1.4.2 Competition

In the digital age, competition can be fierce. Startups must differentiate themselves and continually innovate to stay ahead.

1.4.3 Talent Acquisition

Building a talented team is essential. Attracting and retaining skilled individuals who share your vision is a constant challenge.

1.5 Conclusion

As we delve into the intricacies of startup success in the digital age, it becomes clear that this journey is a dynamic one, filled with opportunities and obstacles. In the chapters that follow, we will explore each aspect of the startup ecosystem, from ideation to growth, and provide insights, strategies, and real-world examples to help startups navigate this exciting but challenging landscape. By mastering the elements discussed in this chapter and adapting to the ever-changing digital environment, startups can increase their chances of achieving success in an era defined by innovation and connectivity.

3

From Idea to Innovation

In the quest for startup success in the digital age, every great journey begins with an idea. While ideas are the seed from which innovation sprouts, turning them into a viable business is a complex and multifaceted process. In this chapter, we'll explore the critical steps and strategies for transforming your initial concept into a tangible, market-ready innovation.

2.1 Ideation and Inspiration

Ideation is the creative process of generating and refining your startup's core concept. It's the point where inspiration meets the practicalities of building a business. Here are some essential aspects to consider:

2.1.1 Identifying a Problem: Successful startups often start with a problem in need of a solution. Look for pain points in your own life or in the lives of others. Solving a real problem can lead to a more sustainable and impactful business.

2.1.2 Market Research: Validate your idea through market research. Understand your target audience, their preferences, and the competitive landscape. This will help you refine your idea and ensure it has a potential market.

2.1.3 Brainstorming: Encourage creative thinking within your team. Hold brainstorming sessions and gather diverse perspectives. Sometimes, the most innovative ideas emerge when multiple minds come together.

2.1.4 Prototyping: Create a prototype or minimum viable product (MVP) to test your idea in the real world. Early feedback is invaluable in refining your concept.

2.2 The Business Plan

With a well-defined idea, it's time to create a comprehensive business plan. A business plan serves as your roadmap, outlining your strategy, goals, and how you intend to reach them.

2.2.1 Executive Summary: Provide a concise overview of your startup, its mission, and key objectives.

2.2.2 Market Analysis: Detail your target market, competitors, and your unique value proposition.

2.2.3 Product or Service Description: Explain in depth what you are offering, how it works, and its benefits.

2.2.4 Marketing and Sales Strategy: Lay out how you plan to attract and retain customers.

2.2.5 Financial Projections: Create financial forecasts, including income statements, cash flow statements, and balance sheets.

2.2.6 Team Structure: Describe your team and their roles.

2.3 Building a Team

A startup's success heavily relies on the people behind it. Building the right team is a critical aspect of turning your idea into a thriving innovation.

2.3.1 Co-Founders: Finding co-founders who complement your skills and share your vision is often essential. A diverse team brings different perspectives to problem-solving.

2.3.2 Hiring: When expanding your team, hire individuals who align with your startup's culture and bring necessary expertise.

2.3.3 Culture: Cultivate a positive and innovative work culture that encourages collaboration and creativity.

2.4 Funding Your Startup

Turning your idea into an innovation often requires financial support. There are various ways to secure funding, including:

2.4.1 Bootstrapping: Using your own savings and revenue to fund the startup.

2.4.2 Angel Investors: High-net-worth individuals who invest in startups in exchange for equity.

2.4.3 Venture Capital: Specialized firms that invest in high-growth startups in exchange for equity.

2.4.4 Crowdfunding: Raising funds from a crowd of individuals who believe in your idea.

2.4.5 Grants and Competitions: Participating in startup competitions and applying for grants can provide non-equity funding.

2.5 Building and Iterating Your Product

With a team and funding in place, it's time to develop your product or service. It's important to follow these key principles:

2.5.1 Agile Development: Embrace an agile development approach, allowing you to adapt to changing market conditions and customer feedback.

2.5.2 User-Centered Design: Prioritize user experience and feedback in your product development process.

2.5.3 Iteration: Continually refine your product based on feedback, emerging technologies, and market trends.

2.6 Protecting Your Innovation

Intellectual property (IP) is valuable. Ensure that you protect your startup's innovations through patents, trademarks, copyrights, or trade secrets.

2.6.1 Patents: Protect novel and non-obvious inventions.

2.6.2 Trademarks: Safeguard your brand and logo.

2.6.3 Copyrights: Protect original works of authorship, such as software code.

2.6.4 Trade Secrets: Keep valuable processes or information confidential.

2.7 Conclusion

The journey from idea to innovation is a crucial phase in the life of a startup. This chapter has outlined the fundamental steps and considerations, from ideation and business planning to assembling the right team, securing funding, and developing your product. The path to startup success is filled with challenges, but with the right strategy and determination, your idea can flourish into a thriving innovation in the digital age. In the next chapter, we'll delve into the art of effective marketing and customer acquisition for startups.

4

Crafting a Compelling Brand and Effective Marketing Strategy

In the competitive landscape of the digital age, startups must not only develop innovative products but also create a strong brand and marketing strategy to connect with their target audience. This chapter explores the art of crafting a compelling brand and building an effective marketing strategy to propel your startup towards success.

3.1 The Power of Branding

3.1.1 Defining Your Brand Identity: Your brand identity encompasses your company's personality, values, mission, and visual elements such as logos and colors. It should resonate with your target audience and be consistent across all touchpoints.

3.1.2 Storytelling: Effective storytelling can humanize your brand and create a deeper connection with customers. Craft a narrative that reflects your journey, values, and the problem you're solving.

3.1.3 Brand Voice: Establish a consistent brand voice and tone in all communications. It should reflect your brand's personality and connect with your audience.

3.2 Understanding Your Target Audience

To create an effective marketing strategy, you must first understand your audience:

3.2.1 Buyer Personas: Develop detailed buyer personas to represent your ideal customers. This includes demographic information, pain points, goals, and preferences.

3.2.2 Market Segmentation: Divide your market into segments with distinct needs and behaviors. Tailor your marketing efforts to each segment.

3.2.3 Customer Journey Mapping: Understand the various stages your customers go through, from awareness to loyalty, and create marketing content to guide them through this journey.

3.3 Online Presence

In the digital age, your online presence is paramount:

3.3.1 Website: Your website is often the first point of contact. Ensure it's user-friendly, visually appealing, and optimized for search engines.

3.3.2 Social Media: Utilize social media platforms to connect with your audience, share content, and build a community.

3.3.3 Content Marketing: Produce valuable content, such as blog posts, videos, and infographics, to educate and engage your audience.

3.4 Search Engine Optimization (SEO)

3.4.1 Keyword Research: Identify keywords relevant to your business and incorporate them into your website and content to improve search engine rankings.

3.4.2 On-Page SEO: Optimize your website's technical aspects, such as page load speed and mobile responsiveness, to enhance user experience and SEO.

3.4.3 Link Building: Build high-quality backlinks to your website to increase authority and visibility in search results.

3.5 Paid Advertising

3.5.1 Pay-Per-Click (PPC): Use platforms like Google Ads and social media advertising to target specific demographics and keywords.

3.5.2 Display Advertising: Create visually appealing banner ads to reach a broader audience.

3.5.3 Retargeting: Use retargeting ads to reach users who have previously visited your website.

3.6 Email Marketing

Email remains a potent tool for customer acquisition and retention:

3.6.1 List Building: Build an email list through sign-up forms on your website and other lead generation tactics.

3.6.2 Personalization: Segment your email list and send personalized content to increase engagement.

3.6.3 Automation: Use email marketing automation to send relevant content and offers at the right time.

3.7 Analytics and Performance Measurement

3.7.1 Key Performance Indicators (KPIs): Define KPIs that align with your business goals, such as website traffic, conversion rates, and customer acquisition cost.

3.7.2 Analytics Tools: Utilize analytics tools like Google Analytics to track and analyze your marketing efforts' performance.

3.7.3 A/B Testing: Experiment with different marketing strategies to determine what works best for your audience.

3.8 Building Community and Loyalty

3.8.1 Social Engagement: Foster a sense of community by engaging with your audience on social media and responding to comments and messages.

3.8.2 Customer Support: Provide exceptional customer support to build trust and loyalty.

3.8.3 Loyalty Programs: Consider loyalty programs or incentives to retain and reward existing customers.

3.9 Conclusion

Crafting a compelling brand and developing an effective marketing strategy are critical elements for startup success in the digital age. Your brand is the emotional connection between your business and your customers, and your marketing strategy is the engine that drives this connection. In the next chapter, we'll explore the intricacies of customer acquisition and growth strategies, helping you expand your startup's reach and impact in the digital landscape.

5

Customer Acquisition and Growth Strategies

In the digital age, attracting and retaining customers is a fundamental aspect of startup success. This chapter delves into customer acquisition and growth strategies, helping you expand your reach, engage your audience, and drive sustainable business growth.

4.1 Customer Acquisition Channels

Effective customer acquisition begins with understanding the various channels through which you can reach your target audience:

4.1.1 Inbound Marketing: Attract customers through valuable content, SEO, and social media marketing.

4.1.2 Outbound Marketing: Utilize strategies like email marketing, paid advertising, and cold outreach to reach potential customers.

4.1.3 Content Marketing: Create informative and engaging content that addresses your customers' needs and pain points.

4.1.4 Social Media: Leverage social media platforms to connect with your audience and promote your products or services.

4.2 Conversion Rate Optimization (CRO)

CRO is the process of improving your website or landing pages to increase the percentage of visitors who take a desired action, such as making a purchase or signing up for a newsletter.

4.2.1 A/B Testing: Experiment with different page elements and content to determine what leads to higher conversions.

4.2.2 Landing Page Optimization: Ensure that your landing pages are tailored to the specific audience and offer a clear value proposition.

4.2.3 User Experience (UX): Optimize the user experience on your website to make it easy for visitors to convert.

4.3 Retention and Customer Relationship Management (CRM)

Retaining existing customers is often more cost-effective than acquiring new ones. Effective retention strategies include:

4.3.1 Personalization: Customize marketing messages and recommendations based on a customer's preferences and behavior.

4.3.2 Customer Support: Provide responsive and helpful customer support to build trust and loyalty.

4.3.3 Loyalty Programs: Reward returning customers with discounts, special offers, or exclusive content.

4.4 Viral Marketing and Referral Programs

Encourage customers to become advocates for your brand and refer others. Viral marketing and referral programs can amplify your growth:

4.4.1 Referral Incentives: Offer rewards to customers who refer friends or family.

4.4.2 Social Sharing: Make it easy for customers to share their positive experiences with your product or service on social media.

4.4.3 User-Generated Content: Encourage customers to create and share content related to your brand.

4.5 Scaling Up

As your startup grows, you'll need to adapt and scale your customer acquisition and growth strategies:

4.5.1 Scalable Marketing Channels: Identify marketing channels that can accommodate growth without a linear increase in costs.

4.5.2 Technology Stack: Invest in tools and technology that can automate and streamline your marketing efforts.

4.5.3 Team Expansion: Hire and train additional team members to handle the increased workload.

4.6 Measuring Success

Key performance indicators (KPIs) are crucial for measuring the success of your customer acquisition and growth strategies:

4.6.1 Customer Acquisition Cost (CAC): Calculate how much it costs to acquire a new customer through each channel.

4.6.2 Customer Lifetime Value (CLV): Determine the value a customer brings to your business over their lifetime.

4.6.3 Conversion Rates: Monitor the percentage of visitors who take the desired actions on your site.

4.7 Conclusion

Customer acquisition and growth strategies are the lifeblood of a startup's journey towards success in the digital age. By understanding your customers, optimizing your marketing efforts, and prioritizing customer retention, you can not only expand your reach but also build a loyal and engaged customer base. In the next chapter, we'll explore the importance of innovation and adaptation in sustaining startup growth and staying relevant in a dynamic digital landscape.

6

Innovation and Adaptation in the Digital Landscape

In the ever-evolving digital landscape, startups must continuously innovate and adapt to stay competitive. This chapter explores the importance of innovation, the strategies for fostering a culture of creativity, and the art of pivoting when necessary to keep your startup thriving.

5.1 The Imperative of Innovation

5.1.1 Staying Relevant: In a rapidly changing environment, maintaining relevance and competitiveness hinges on your ability to innovate. Embrace new technologies, trends, and customer demands.

5.1.2 Differentiation: Innovation sets you apart from competitors. Unique products, services, or approaches attract customers and investors.

5.1.3 Growth: Continuous innovation can lead to expanded product lines, new markets, and sustainable growth.

5.2 Fostering a Culture of Creativity

5.2.1 Encourage Experimentation: Create an environment where employees feel comfortable trying new things and taking calculated risks.

5.2.2 Diversity: Diverse teams often bring diverse perspectives, which can lead to more innovative ideas.

5.2.3 Open Communication: Foster open and transparent communication within the organization, encouraging the sharing of ideas and feedback.

5.2.4 Learning Mindset: Promote a culture of continuous learning and improvement.

5.3 Embracing Technological Advancements

5.3.1 Keeping Up: Stay informed about emerging technologies that can disrupt or enhance your industry.

5.3.2 Technology Partnerships: Collaborate with tech partners to access cutting-edge solutions without having to build everything in-house.

5.3.3 Research and Development: Allocate resources to research and development to keep your products or services on the cutting edge.

5.4 Adapting to Market Changes

5.4.1 Monitoring Trends: Keep a vigilant eye on market trends, customer feedback, and competitive shifts.

5.4.2 Pivoting: Be willing to pivot your business model or strategy when market conditions require it. This may include adjusting your product, target audience, or marketing approach.

5.4.3 Agility: Develop an agile organizational structure that can quickly respond to changing circumstances.

5.5 Customer-Centric Innovation

5.5.1 Customer Feedback: Regularly solicit and act upon feedback from customers to address their needs and preferences.

5.5.2 Co-Creation: Involve customers in the product development process to ensure that what you're building aligns with their expectations.

5.5.3 User Experience (UX): Prioritize a seamless and enjoyable customer experience as part of your innovation efforts.

5.6 Sustainability and Responsible Innovation

5.6.1 Environmental Responsibility: Consider sustainability and eco-friendly practices in your innovation processes.

5.6.2 Ethical Considerations: Ensure your innovations align with ethical and social responsibilities.

5.6.3 Regulatory Compliance: Stay up-to-date with relevant regulations and standards that might impact your innovations.

5.7 Measuring and Assessing Innovation

5.7.1 Key Metrics: Use key performance indicators (KPIs) to measure the success and impact of your innovations.

5.7.2 Feedback Loops: Establish feedback mechanisms to assess how well your innovations are received by customers and the market.

5.7.3 Continuous Improvement: Learn from both successful and unsuccessful innovations to continually improve your processes.

5.8 Conclusion

Innovation and adaptation are essential to staying competitive and relevant in the digital landscape. By fostering a culture of creativity, embracing technology, and staying attuned to market changes, your startup can thrive in an ever-evolving environment. In the next chapter, we'll explore the critical element of financial management and sustainability, ensuring that your startup can weather the challenges and uncertainties of the digital age.

7

Financial Management and Sustainability

Financial management is a cornerstone of startup success in the digital age. This chapter delves into the importance of sound financial practices, including budgeting, cash flow management, and sustainable growth strategies, to ensure your startup not only survives but thrives in a dynamic and competitive landscape.

6.1 The Foundation of Financial Health

6.1.1 Budgeting: Create a detailed budget that outlines your expenses and revenue projections. Regularly review and adjust it as needed.

6.1.2 Cash Flow Management: Monitor and manage your cash flow to ensure that you have the funds needed to cover operating expenses, pay suppliers, and invest in growth.

6.1.3 Financial Transparency: Maintain clear and transparent financial records, and consider utilizing accounting software or services.

6.2 Funding Sources

6.2.1 Bootstrapping: Using your own savings and revenue to fund the startup.

6.2.2 Angel Investors: Seek investments from individuals who provide capital in exchange for equity.

6.2.3 Venture Capital: Attract venture capital from firms specializing in high-growth startups.

6.2.4 Crowdfunding: Raise funds from a crowd of individuals who believe in your idea.

6.2.5 Grants and Competitions: Participate in startup competitions and apply for grants to secure non-equity funding.

6.3 Sustainable Growth Strategies

6.3.1 Incremental Growth: Avoid overexpansion and focus on steady, controlled growth to minimize risks.

6.3.2 Profitability: Prioritize profitability over rapid expansion, ensuring that revenue covers expenses.

6.3.3 Diversification: Explore opportunities to diversify your product or service offerings and revenue streams.

6.4 Cost Management

6.4.1 Lean Approach: Adopt a lean methodology, minimizing waste and unnecessary expenditures.

6.4.2 Vendor Relationships: Negotiate with suppliers and vendors to secure favorable terms and pricing.

6.4.3 Outsourcing: Consider outsourcing non-core functions to reduce costs and improve efficiency.

6.5 Risk Management

6.5.1 Risk Assessment: Identify and assess potential risks to your startup, including market shifts, competition, and financial instability.

6.5.2 Risk Mitigation: Develop strategies to mitigate identified risks, such as diversification, insurance, or contingency plans.

6.5.3 Legal and Regulatory Compliance: Stay informed about and comply with legal and regulatory requirements to avoid potential liabilities.

6.6 Long-Term Financial Planning

6.6.1 Financial Forecasting: Use historical data and market analysis to forecast your startup's financial performance over time.

6.6.2 Exit Strategies: Consider potential exit strategies, such as acquisition, merger, or IPO, and align your financial planning with your long-term goals.

6.6.3 Tax Planning: Work with tax professionals to optimize your tax strategy and minimize liabilities.

6.7 Measuring Financial Success

6.7.1 Key Financial Metrics: Monitor key financial metrics such as revenue, expenses, profit margins, and return on investment (ROI).

6.7.2 Performance Benchmarks: Compare your financial performance to industry benchmarks to assess your startup's health and competitiveness.

6.7.3 Reporting and Analysis: Regularly review financial reports and engage in financial analysis to make informed decisions.

6.8 Conclusion

Effective financial management and sustainability practices are critical for ensuring your startup's success and longevity. By establishing a solid financial foundation, securing the right funding, and implementing sustainable growth strategies, you can navigate the financial challenges of the digital age and position your startup for lasting success. In the next chapter, we'll explore the human aspect of startups, including team dynamics, leadership, and company culture.

8

Nurturing Team Dynamics, Leadership, and Company Culture

In the digital age, startups are not just about products and technology; they are also about the people who drive innovation and growth. This chapter delves into the critical human aspects of startups, including fostering effective team dynamics, leadership development, and the cultivation of a positive company culture.

7.1 Building the Right Team

7.1.1 Hiring: Selecting the right individuals is pivotal. Prioritize candidates who share your startup's values and have the skills and mindset needed for success.

7.1.2 Team Diversity: A diverse team can bring varied perspectives and creativity to problem-solving.

7.1.3 Culture Fit: Ensure that new team members align with your startup's culture and mission.

7.2 Effective Team Dynamics

7.2.1 Communication: Encourage open, transparent, and constructive communication among team members.

7.2.2 Collaboration: Promote a collaborative environment where individuals work together to achieve common goals.

7.2.3 Accountability: Hold team members accountable for their responsibilities and contributions.

7.3 Leadership Development

7.3.1 Lead by Example: Effective leaders set the tone for the organization through their actions, work ethic, and dedication.

7.3.2 Continuous Learning: Encourage leadership to continually develop their skills and knowledge.

7.3.3 Empowerment: Empower leaders and team members to make decisions and take ownership of their roles.

7.4 Company Culture

7.4.1 Defined Values: Establish clear values that guide the behavior and decisions of all team members.

7.4.2 Employee Well-being: Prioritize the well-being of your team, including work-life balance, mental health, and job satisfaction.

7.4.3 Recognition and Rewards: Recognize and reward employees for their contributions and achievements.

NURTURING TEAM DYNAMICS, LEADERSHIP, AND COMPANY CULTURE

7.5 Conflict Resolution

7.5.1 Proactive Approach: Address conflicts promptly and proactively to prevent escalation.

7.5.2 Mediation: Use mediation techniques when conflicts arise, involving a neutral third party if necessary.

7.5.3 Learning from Conflict: Treat conflicts as opportunities for growth and learning within the team.

7.6 Leadership Styles

7.6.1 Transformational Leadership: Inspire and motivate team members to reach their full potential.

7.6.2 Servant Leadership: Prioritize the needs and growth of team members.

7.6.3 Adaptive Leadership: Adjust leadership approaches based on the specific needs of the team and the context.

7.7 Company Values and Mission

7.7.1 Values Alignment: Ensure that the values of your team align with your startup's mission and objectives.

7.7.2 Mission Communication: Clearly communicate your startup's mission to all team members, so they understand the larger purpose.

7.7.3 Mission-Driven Work: Encourage team members to connect their work to the broader mission and goals of the organization.

7.8 Conclusion

The human element of startups is instrumental in shaping their culture, effectiveness, and overall success. By nurturing effective team dynamics, fostering leadership development, and cultivating a positive company culture, startups can harness the full potential of their team members and create a work environment that fuels innovation and growth. In the next chapter, we'll explore the significance of adaptability and resilience in navigating the unpredictable journey of startup entrepreneurship.

9

Adaptability and Resilience in Startup Entrepreneurship

In the ever-changing landscape of startup entrepreneurship, adaptability and resilience are the keys to weathering challenges and emerging stronger. This chapter delves into the importance of these traits and provides strategies for developing them to navigate the unpredictable journey of building and scaling a startup.

8.1 The Dynamic Nature of Entrepreneurship

8.1.1 Uncertainty: Accept that uncertainty is inherent in entrepreneurship, and embrace it as an opportunity for growth.

8.1.2 Market Shifts: Be prepared to pivot when market conditions change or new opportunities emerge.

8.1.3 Learning Mindset: Develop a mindset that views challenges and setbacks as learning experiences.

8.2 Embracing Change

8.2.1 Flexible Strategies: Develop adaptable strategies that can evolve to meet new circumstances.

8.2.2 Open-Mindedness: Be open to feedback, new ideas, and different perspectives.

8.2.3 Experimentation: Encourage a culture of experimentation, allowing for innovation and evolution.

8.3 Handling Setbacks

8.3.1 Resilience: Develop the ability to bounce back from setbacks and failures.

8.3.2 Support Networks: Surround yourself with mentors, advisors, and a supportive team to help you navigate tough times.

8.3.3 Mindfulness and Well-being: Prioritize self-care, mindfulness, and well-being to build resilience and mental strength.

8.4 Risk Management

8.4.1 Risk Assessment: Continuously assess and manage risks to minimize the impact of unexpected challenges.

8.4.2 Contingency Planning: Develop contingency plans to respond to potential risks and disruptions.

8.4.3 Insurance: Consider appropriate insurance coverage to protect against unexpected events.

8.5 Fostering a Resilient Team

8.5.1 Leadership Example: Lead by example, demonstrating resilience and adaptability to inspire your team.

8.5.2 Training: Provide training and support to help team members develop their own resilience.

8.5.3 Team-Building: Foster a sense of community and mutual support within the team.

8.6 Seeking Opportunities in Challenges

8.6.1 Innovating Through Challenges: Use challenges as opportunities to innovate and improve your products or services.

8.6.2 Market Gaps: Identify market gaps created by change and adapt your offerings to fill those gaps.

8.6.3 Resilience as a Competitive Advantage: Position resilience as a competitive advantage that sets your startup apart.

8.7 Measuring Adaptability and Resilience

8.7.1 Key Performance Indicators (KPIs): Use KPIs to track the adaptability and resilience of your startup and team.

8.7.2 Feedback and Self-Assessment: Regularly seek feedback and self-assess to identify areas for improvement.

8.7.3 Adaptation Success Stories: Celebrate instances of successful adaptation and resilience within your startup.

8.8 Conclusion

The journey of startup entrepreneurship is marked by twists and turns, and the ability to adapt and remain resilient is crucial for success. By embracing change, learning from setbacks, and fostering a resilient team, startups can navigate the unpredictability of entrepreneurship and emerge stronger on the other side. In the next chapter, we'll explore the broader ecosystem of support and resources available to startups, from incubators and accelerators to mentorship and networking opportunities.

10

Navigating the Startup Ecosystem

Startup success is not a solitary endeavor; it thrives within a broader ecosystem of support, resources, and collaboration. This chapter explores the significance of the startup ecosystem and how to leverage it to your advantage, including the role of incubators, accelerators, mentorship, and networking opportunities.

9.1 The Importance of the Ecosystem

9.1.1 Collaboration: The startup ecosystem fosters collaboration and knowledge sharing, which can lead to innovation and growth.

9.1.2 Resources: It provides access to vital resources such as funding, mentorship, and industry expertise.

9.1.3 Validation: Participation in the ecosystem can validate your startup's viability and potential.

9.2 Incubators and Accelerators

9.2.1 Incubators: Incubators offer early-stage startups support, resources, and mentorship to help them develop and refine their ideas.

9.2.2 Accelerators: Accelerators provide startups with a structured program, typically culminating in a demo day to pitch to potential investors.

9.2.3 Selection Process: Participating in an incubator or accelerator often involves a competitive selection process.

9.3 Mentorship

9.3.1 Mentor-Mentee Relationships: Mentorship connects experienced entrepreneurs with those who are just starting, offering guidance, support, and valuable insights.

9.3.2 Mentoring Networks: Join mentoring networks and platforms that can connect you with potential mentors.

9.3.3 Reverse Mentorship: Consider the benefits of reverse mentorship, where younger team members mentor senior individuals on technological and market trends.

9.4 Networking Opportunities

9.4.1 Networking Events: Attend startup and industry-specific events, conferences, and meetups to connect with potential partners, investors, and customers.

9.4.2 Online Communities: Engage in online forums, social media groups, and platforms to connect with other entrepreneurs and industry professionals.

9.4.3 Alumni Networks: Leverage the power of alumni networks from incubators, accelerators, and educational institutions.

9.5 Access to Funding

9.5.1 Angel Investors: Engage with angel investors who can provide early-stage funding and valuable advice.

9.5.2 Venture Capital: Seek venture capital firms specializing in startups that align with your industry and growth stage.

9.5.3 Crowdfunding: Explore crowdfunding platforms to secure funding from a crowd of supporters.

9.6 Government and Nonprofit Support

9.6.1 Grants and Subsidies: Investigate government grants, subsidies, and programs for startups in your region.

9.6.2 Nonprofit Organizations: Connect with nonprofit organizations that offer resources and support to startups.

9.6.3 Business Incubation Centers: Explore local business incubation centers that provide physical space, mentorship, and networking opportunities.

9.7 Measuring Success within the Ecosystem

9.7.1 Partnership Outcomes: Evaluate the success of partnerships and collaborations within the ecosystem.

9.7.2 Investment Opportunities: Assess the number and quality of investment opportunities that arise from your ecosystem connections.

9.7.3 Knowledge Gained: Measure the knowledge and skills your team acquires through mentorship and networking.

9.8 Conclusion

The startup ecosystem is a rich source of support and opportunity, providing collaboration, resources, mentorship, and networking that can propel your startup to new heights. By actively engaging with the ecosystem, you can leverage these resources to accelerate your growth and increase your chances of success. In the final chapter of this book, we'll reflect on the overarching principles and strategies for startup success, bringing together all the key elements discussed throughout the book.

11

The Path to Startup Success: Key Principles and Strategies

In the journey of startup entrepreneurship, success is the culmination of various strategies and principles. This final chapter brings together the key elements discussed throughout the book and provides a comprehensive overview of the principles and strategies that underpin startup success in the digital age.

10.1 Vision and Clarity

10.1.1 Clear Mission: Define a clear and compelling mission that serves as your startup's guiding light.

10.1.2 Visionary Leadership: Lead with vision and inspire your team to rally behind a common goal.

10.2 Innovation and Adaptation

10.2.1 Continuous Innovation: Prioritize innovation and remain open to evolving your product or service.

10.2.2 Adaptability: Be prepared to pivot when market conditions change or new opportunities arise.

10.3 Customer-Centric Focus

10.3.1 Customer Understanding: Develop a deep understanding of your customers' needs, pain points, and preferences.

10.3.2 Exceptional User Experience: Prioritize user experience to create a loyal customer base.

10.4 Financial Management

10.4.1 Budgeting and Cash Flow: Establish a sound financial foundation through effective budgeting and cash flow management.

10.4.2 Sustainable Growth: Focus on sustainable growth and profitability over rapid expansion.

10.5 Team Dynamics and Leadership

10.5.1 Building the Right Team: Select team members who share your values and bring diverse skills to the table.

10.5.2 Effective Leadership: Lead by example, support your team's growth, and cultivate a positive company culture.

10.6 Adaptability and Resilience

10.6.1 Embracing Change: Embrace change as an opportunity for growth and adapt your strategies accordingly.

10.6.2 Handling Setbacks: Build resilience to bounce back from challenges and setbacks.

10.7 Navigating the Ecosystem

10.7.1 Utilizing Resources: Leverage the startup ecosystem for mentorship, networking, and funding.

10.7.2 Continuous Learning: Engage in continuous learning and remain open to feedback and new ideas.

10.8 Measuring Success

10.8.1 Key Performance Indicators (KPIs): Use KPIs to assess the success and impact of your strategies and initiatives.

10.8.2 Feedback and Reflection: Regularly seek feedback and engage in self-assessment to identify areas for improvement.

10.9 Conclusion

The path to startup success is challenging and dynamic, but by adhering to these principles and strategies, you can navigate the complexities of the digital age with confidence. Remember that success is not a destination but an ongoing journey of growth, adaptation, and innovation. Stay true to your vision, embrace change, and continue to learn and evolve. Your startup's success is a testament to your determination, vision, and the transformative power of entrepreneurship in the digital age.

12

Beyond Startup Success: Sustaining and Scaling

Reaching startup success is a significant achievement, but the journey doesn't end there. This chapter explores the essential strategies and considerations for sustaining your success and scaling your startup for long-term growth in the ever-evolving digital landscape.

11.1 The Evolution of Success

11.1.1 Sustainable Success: Define what success means for your startup beyond the initial phase, considering long-term sustainability and growth.

11.1.2 Continuous Improvement: Cultivate a culture of constant improvement and innovation to remain competitive.

11.1.3 Measuring Progress: Establish key performance indicators (KPIs) that align with your long-term goals and monitor progress over time.

11.2 Scaling Strategies

11.2.1 Scalability Assessment: Evaluate your product, infrastructure, and processes to ensure they can handle increased demand.

11.2.2 Market Expansion: Explore opportunities for geographic or demographic expansion to reach new customer segments.

11.2.3 Strategic Partnerships: Consider partnerships with other businesses to access new markets, technologies, or resources.

11.3 Talent and Leadership

11.3.1 Team Growth: Scale your team strategically to support increased demand and expansion.

11.3.2 Leadership Development: Invest in leadership training and development to ensure strong, adaptable leadership as your startup scales.

11.3.3 Remote and Distributed Teams: Consider remote and distributed teams to access a wider talent pool and optimize cost management.

11.4 Technology and Infrastructure

11.4.1 Tech Stack Evolution: Continually upgrade and adapt your technology stack to meet growing demands and market trends.

11.4.2 Scalable Infrastructure: Invest in scalable infrastructure that can handle increased traffic and data requirements.

11.4.3 Data Security: Prioritize robust data security measures to protect your startup and your customers.

11.5 Customer Retention and Expansion

11.5.1 Customer Loyalty Programs: Implement loyalty programs to reward and retain existing customers.

11.5.2 Cross-Selling and Upselling: Explore opportunities to sell additional products or services to existing customers.

11.5.3 Customer Feedback: Continue to gather and act upon customer feedback to improve your offerings.

11.6 Regulatory and Compliance Considerations

11.6.1 Legal and Compliance: Stay updated with relevant laws and regulations that may impact your startup's operations and scaling efforts.

11.6.2 Ethical Practices: Uphold ethical business practices and social responsibility as you expand your reach.

11.6.3 Risk Management: Continuously assess and mitigate potential risks associated with scaling.

11.7 Financial Management in Scaling

11.7.1 Budget Reallocation: Reallocate your budget to prioritize areas critical for scaling, such as marketing, technology, and talent acquisition.

11.7.2 Investment Strategies: Seek funding or investment opportunities that align with your scaling goals.

11.7.3 Performance Metrics: Monitor the financial performance of your scaling efforts through relevant metrics.

11.8 Sustainable Growth Mindset

11.8.1 Balance and Stability: Strive for a balanced approach between growth and stability to avoid overextending your startup.

11.8.2 Environmental Responsibility: Continue to integrate sustainable and eco-friendly practices into your operations.

11.8.3 Giving Back: Consider philanthropic and community initiatives as your startup scales.

11.9 Conclusion

The path beyond startup success is filled with new challenges and opportunities. Sustaining and scaling your startup requires a focused, strategic approach, with a commitment to continuous innovation and adaptation. Stay true to your mission and values, maintain a strong team and leadership, and remain dedicated to creating a positive impact in the digital age. Your startup's journey is a testament to your vision, determination, and commitment to making a difference in the world.

13

Looking Ahead: Future Trends and Possibilities

In the fast-paced world of startup entrepreneurship, staying ahead of the curve is essential. This final chapter explores some of the future trends, emerging technologies, and possibilities that may shape the landscape for startups in the coming years, providing insights into the opportunities and challenges that lie ahead.

12.1 Tech Trends

12.1.1 Artificial Intelligence (AI): AI and machine learning will continue to revolutionize industries, providing opportunities for startups to develop innovative applications and solutions.

12.1.2 Blockchain: The adoption of blockchain technology will expand, creating new possibilities for secure transactions, smart contracts, and digital identity verification.

12.1.3 Internet of Things (IoT): IoT devices will become more integrated into daily life, opening doors for startups in fields like smart homes, healthcare, and industrial applications.

12.2 Sustainability and ESG

12.2.1 Environmental Sustainability: Green startups will play an increasingly important role in addressing environmental challenges and creating eco-friendly solutions.

12.2.2 Social Responsibility: Startups with a strong focus on social impact and responsible business practices will gain recognition and support.

12.2.3 Governance and Transparency: Emphasis on governance and transparency will shape the future of startups and their interactions with stakeholders.

12.3 Remote Work and Distributed Teams

12.3.1 Remote Work Culture: Remote work will become the norm for many startups, offering flexibility and access to global talent.

12.3.2 Challenges of Remote Work: Startups will need to address challenges such as team collaboration, security, and employee well-being in a remote work environment.

12.3.3 Tools and Platforms: The development of tools and platforms for remote work will continue to grow, enhancing the efficiency of distributed teams.

12.4 Data Privacy and Security

12.4.1 Data Protection Laws: Stricter data privacy regulations will continue to impact how startups collect, store, and manage customer data.

12.4.2 Cybersecurity: The need for robust cybersecurity measures will remain critical to protect against data breaches and threats.

12.4.3 Privacy-Focused Technologies: Privacy-focused technologies and solutions will gain traction as consumers seek more control over their data.

12.5 Emerging Industries

12.5.1 Space Exploration: The space industry will present new opportunities for startups in satellite technology, asteroid mining, and space tourism.

12.5.2 Healthcare Innovation: Healthcare startups will continue to focus on telemedicine, personalized medicine, and biotechnology.

12.5.3 Clean Energy: Startups in clean energy, renewable resources, and sustainable transportation will lead the way in addressing environmental challenges.

12.6 Ethical AI and Automation

12.6.1 Ethical AI: A growing focus on ethical considerations in AI and automation will shape the development of responsible and unbiased algorithms.

12.6.2 Human-AI Collaboration: The interaction between humans and AI will become more symbiotic, opening new opportunities for startups in human-AI partnerships.

12.6.3 AI Regulation: As AI technology advances, governments and organizations will seek to regulate its use, creating both challenges and opportunities for startups.

12.7 Conclusion

LOOKING AHEAD: FUTURE TRENDS AND POSSIBILITIES

The future of startups is brimming with possibilities and challenges. Staying attuned to emerging trends, embracing technological innovations, and maintaining a commitment to ethics and sustainability will be vital for success. The journey of entrepreneurship in the digital age is an ever-evolving one, and your startup's ability to adapt and seize opportunities will determine its place in the future of innovation and impact. Embrace change, remain resilient, and continue to innovate as you navigate the exciting path ahead.

In this comprehensive book, we've explored the multifaceted world of startup entrepreneurship in the digital age. Here's a summary of the key chapters and their insights:

Chapter 1: Startup Success in the Digital Age
  - Introduced the digital age's impact on entrepreneurship.
  - Emphasized the importance of a clear vision, mission, and value proposition.
  - Highlighted the significance of a strong startup culture and values.

Chapter 2: The Fundamentals of Starting Up
  - Explored the initial steps of turning an idea into a viable startup.
  - Addressed the importance of market research and validation.
  - Discussed the legal and financial considerations when launching a startup.

Chapter 3: The Power of Marketing and Branding
  - Delved into the role of marketing and branding in attracting customers.
  - Covered strategies for building a strong brand identity.
  - Highlighted the value of customer segmentation and targeting.

Chapter 4: Building and Managing a High-Performing Team
  - Explored the pivotal role of team dynamics and leadership in startup success.
  - Discussed recruitment, team development, and fostering a positive company culture.

- Emphasized the importance of diversity and inclusion within the team.

Chapter 5: Innovation and Adaptation in the Digital Landscape
- Underlined the necessity of continuous innovation for staying competitive.
- Explored strategies for fostering a culture of creativity.
- Discussed adapting to market changes and prioritizing customer-centric innovation.

Chapter 6: Financial Management and Sustainability
- Emphasized sound financial practices, including budgeting and cash flow management.
- Explored various funding sources and sustainable growth strategies.
- Discussed cost management, risk mitigation, and long-term financial planning.

Chapter 7: Nurturing Team Dynamics, Leadership, and Company Culture
- Focused on the human element in startups, including team building, effective leadership, and fostering a positive company culture.
- Addressed conflict resolution, leadership styles, and the alignment of company values and mission.

Chapter 8: Adaptability and Resilience in Startup Entrepreneurship
- Highlighted the importance of adaptability and resilience in navigating the unpredictable startup journey.
- Explored strategies for embracing change and handling setbacks.
- Discussed risk management, leadership, and learning from challenges.

Chapter 9: Navigating the Startup Ecosystem
- Explored the broader ecosystem of support, resources, and collaboration for startups.
- Discussed the roles of incubators, accelerators, mentorship, and networking opportunities.

- Highlighted the importance of accessing funding and government and nonprofit support.

Chapter 10: The Path to Startup Success: Key Principles and Strategies
- Brought together the key principles and strategies discussed in previous chapters.
- Emphasized the continuous journey of growth, adaptation, and innovation in startup success.

Chapter 11: Beyond Startup Success: Sustaining and Scaling
- Explored strategies for sustaining success and scaling a startup for long-term growth.
- Covered talent acquisition, technology and infrastructure, customer retention, regulatory compliance, and sustainable growth.

Chapter 12: Looking Ahead: Future Trends and Possibilities
- Examined future trends and emerging technologies that may shape the startup landscape.
- Discussed areas such as tech trends, sustainability, remote work, data privacy, emerging industries, and ethical AI.

This book serves as a comprehensive guide for aspiring and current startup entrepreneurs, providing insights into the critical aspects of building, growing, and sustaining successful startups in the dynamic digital age. It emphasizes the importance of innovation, adaptability, team dynamics, financial management, leadership, and a strong connection to the broader startup ecosystem. The future trends discussed in the final chapter offer a glimpse into the exciting possibilities and challenges awaiting startups as they continue to make their mark in the world of entrepreneurship.

www.ingramcontent.com/pod-product-compliance
Lightning Source LLC
LaVergne TN
LVHW010435070526
838199LV00066B/6039